AuthentikMinds Creative Space

Copyright AuthentikMinds 2018. All Rights Reserved.

Author : Jeyanthi Ramamoorthy

ISBN-13: 978-1984071736
ISBN-10: 1984071734

KIWI GARDEN Belongs to

_____

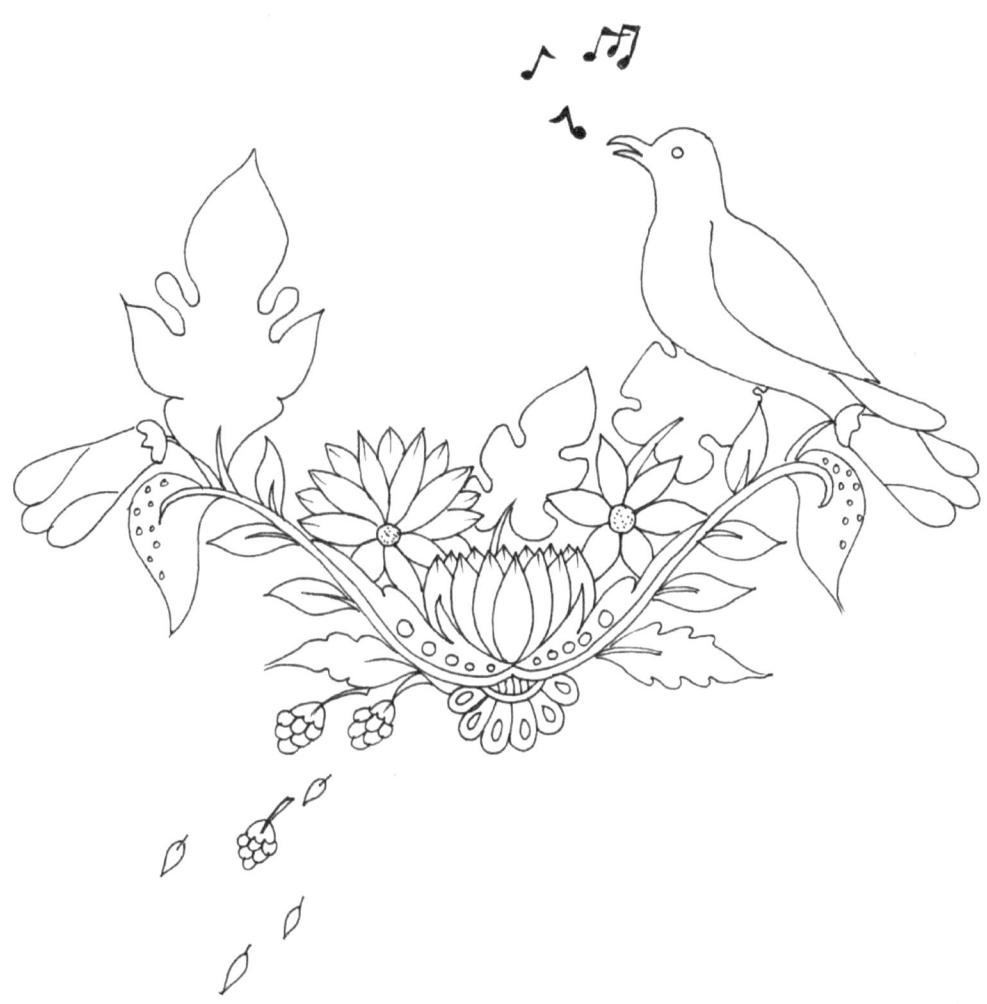

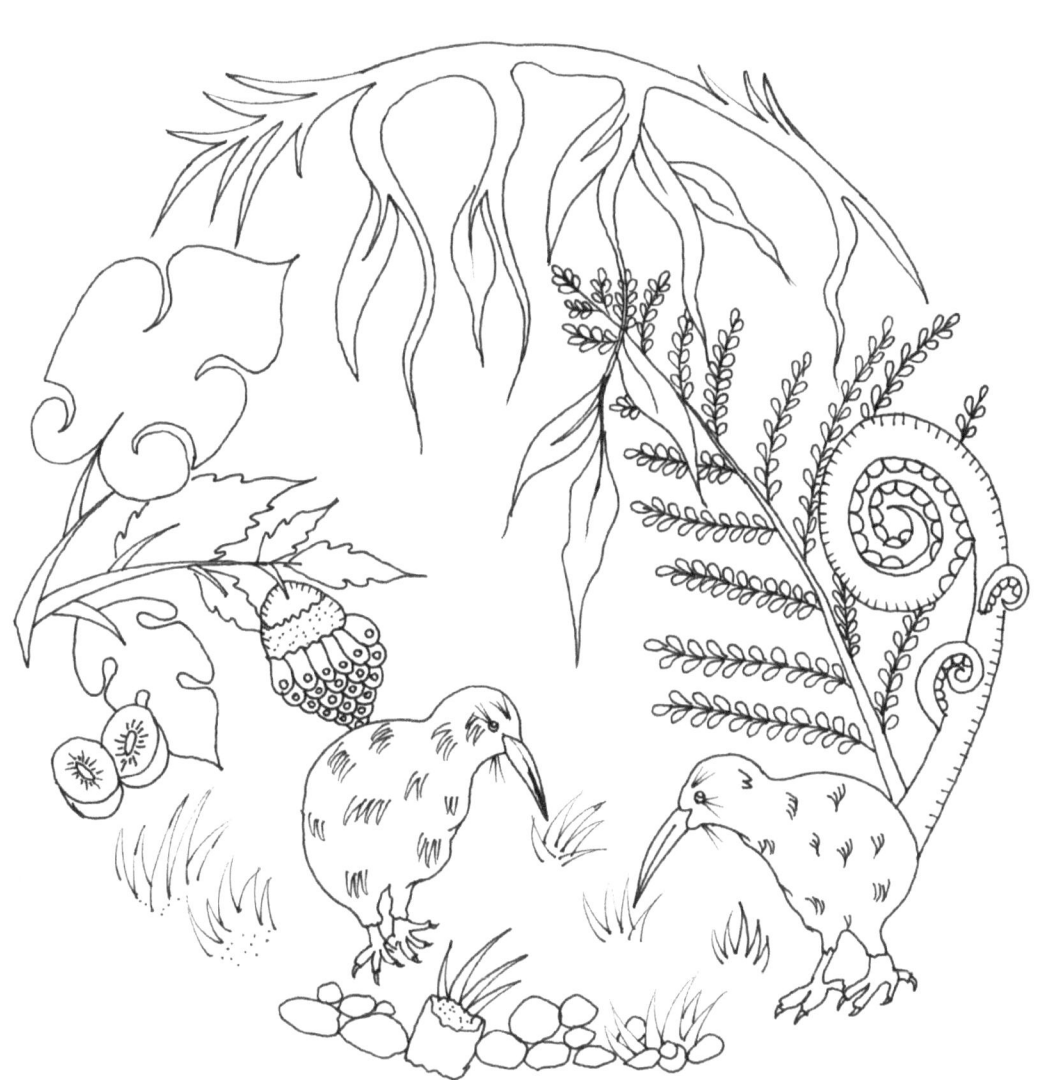

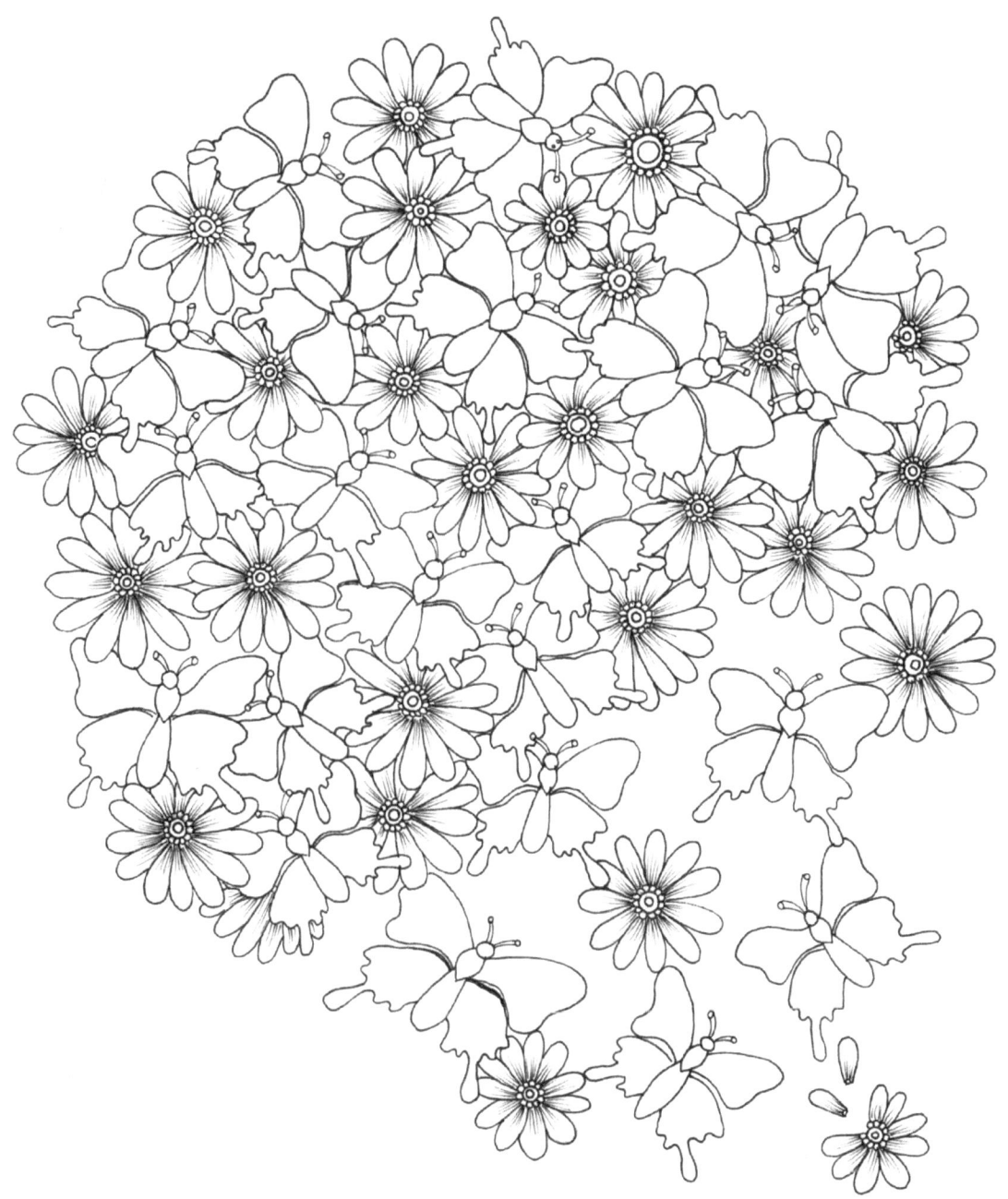

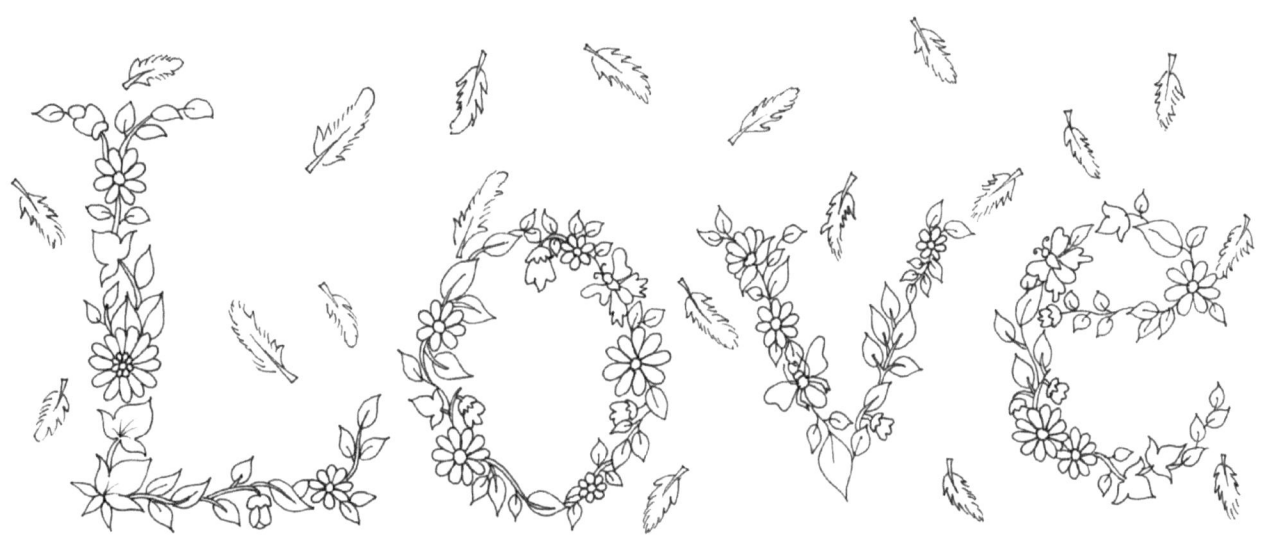

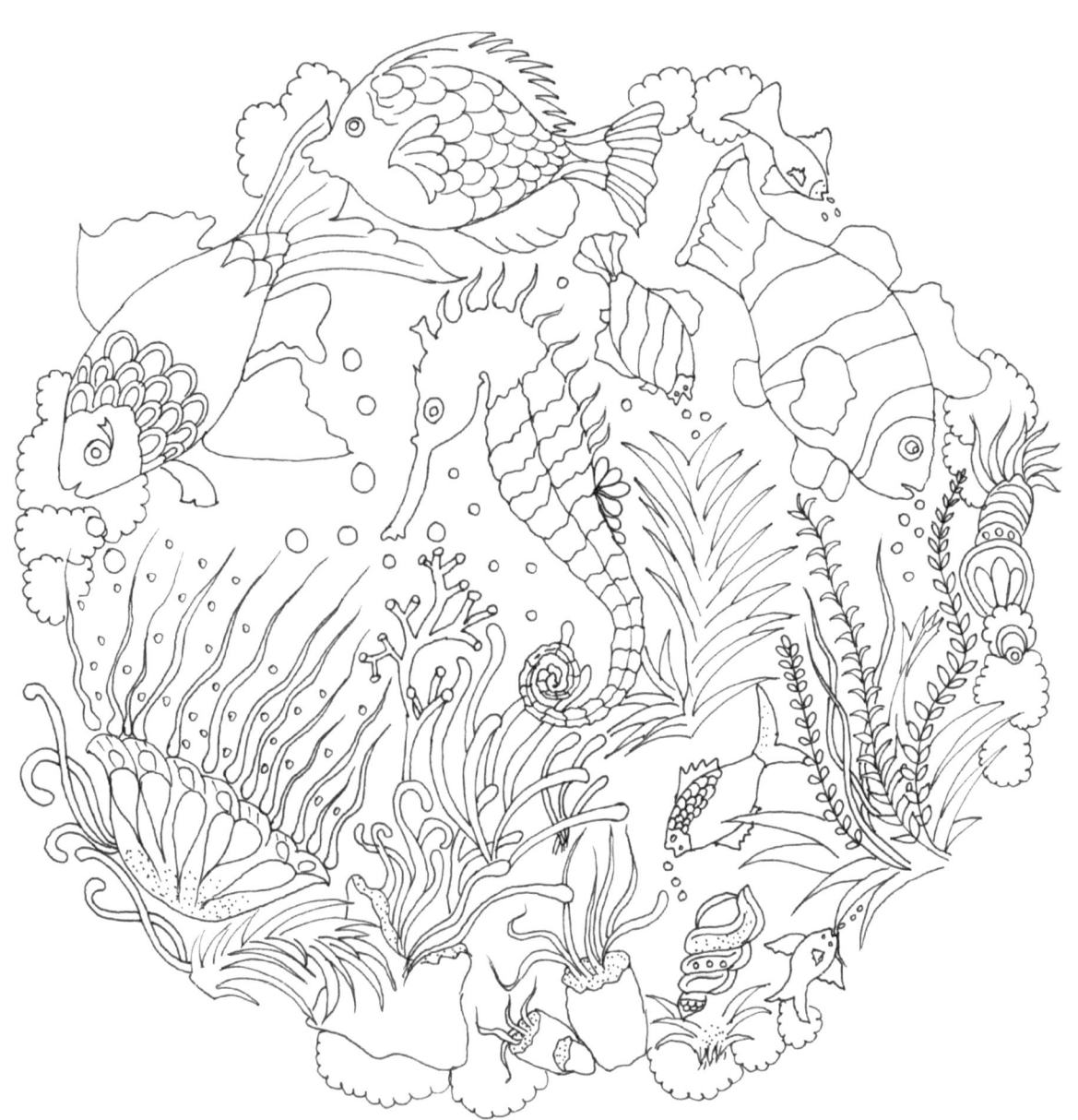

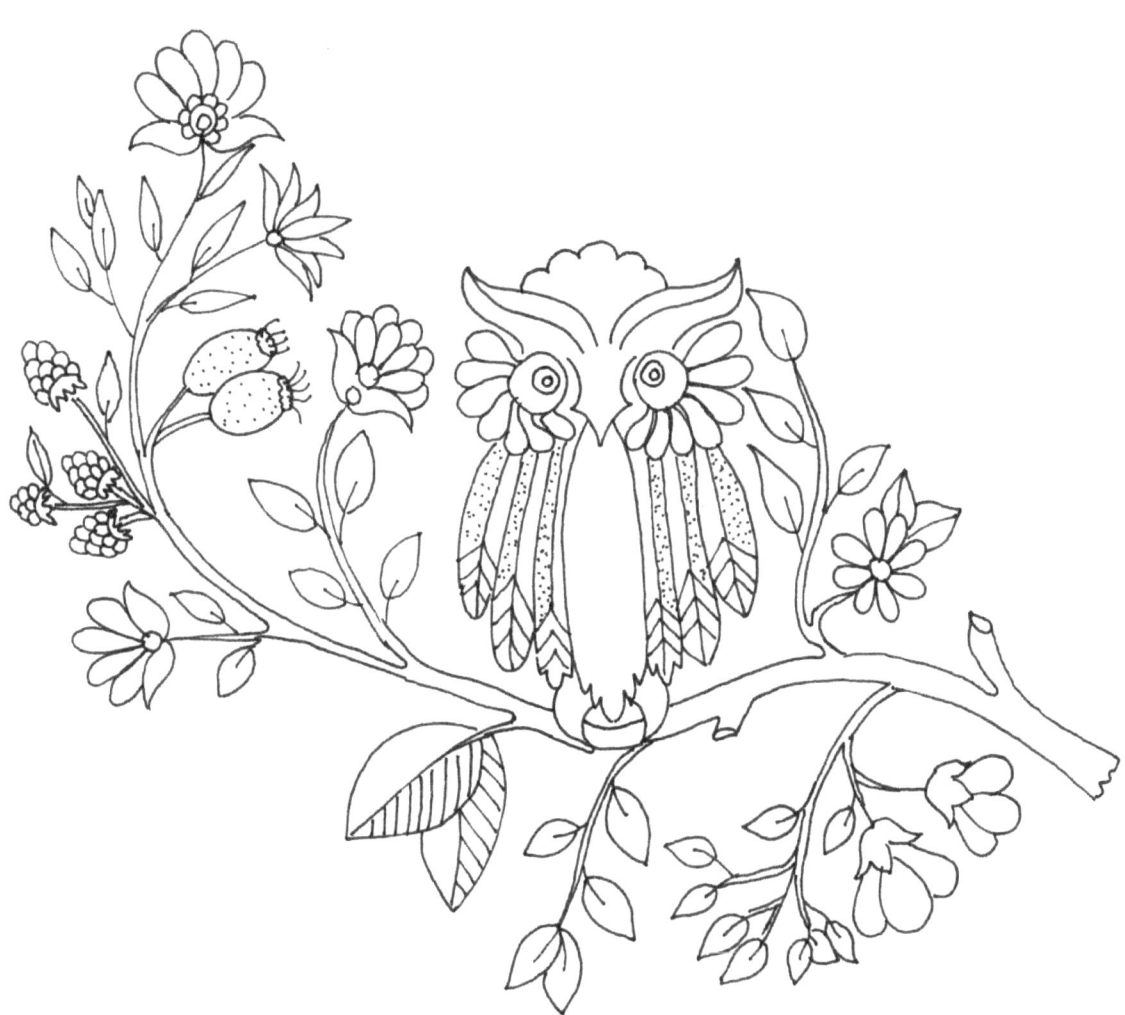

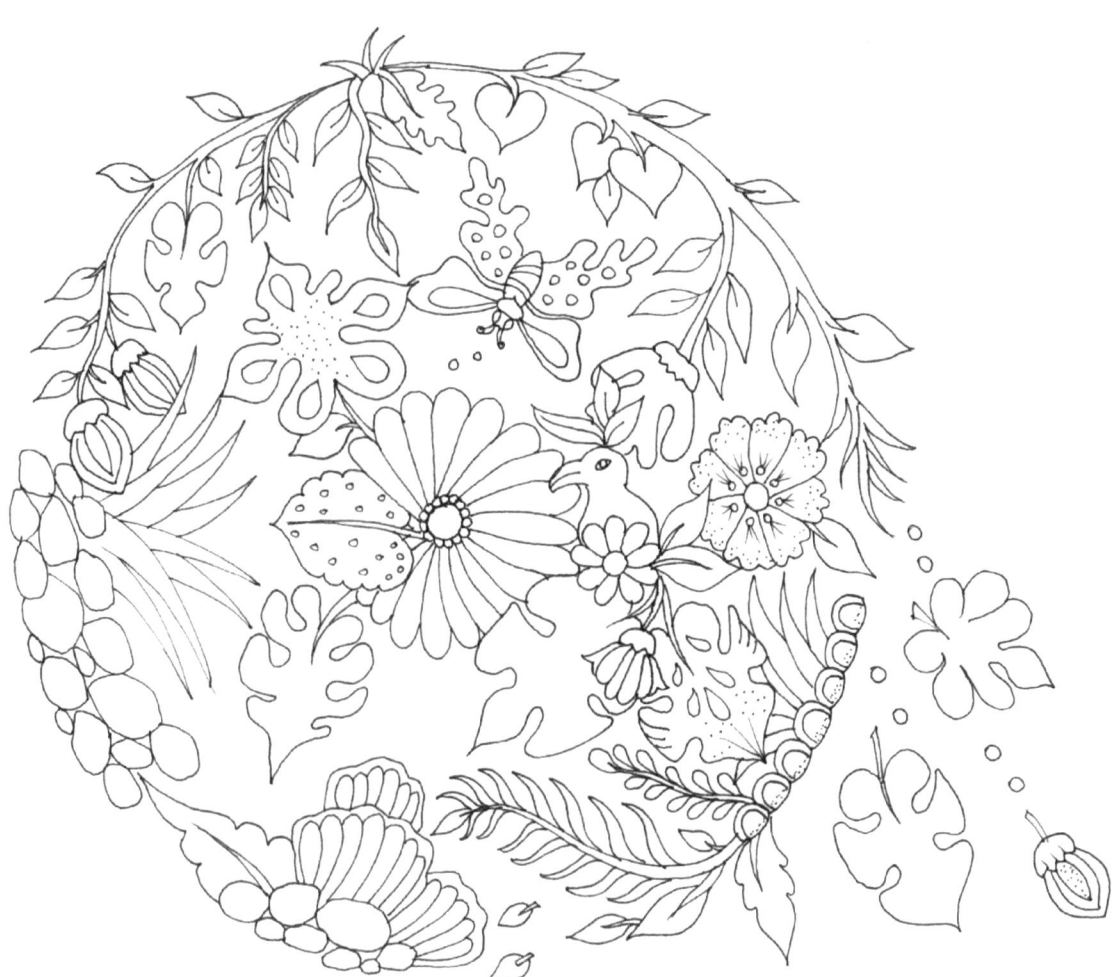

Have fun with your Intelligence through colouring

#Authentikminds

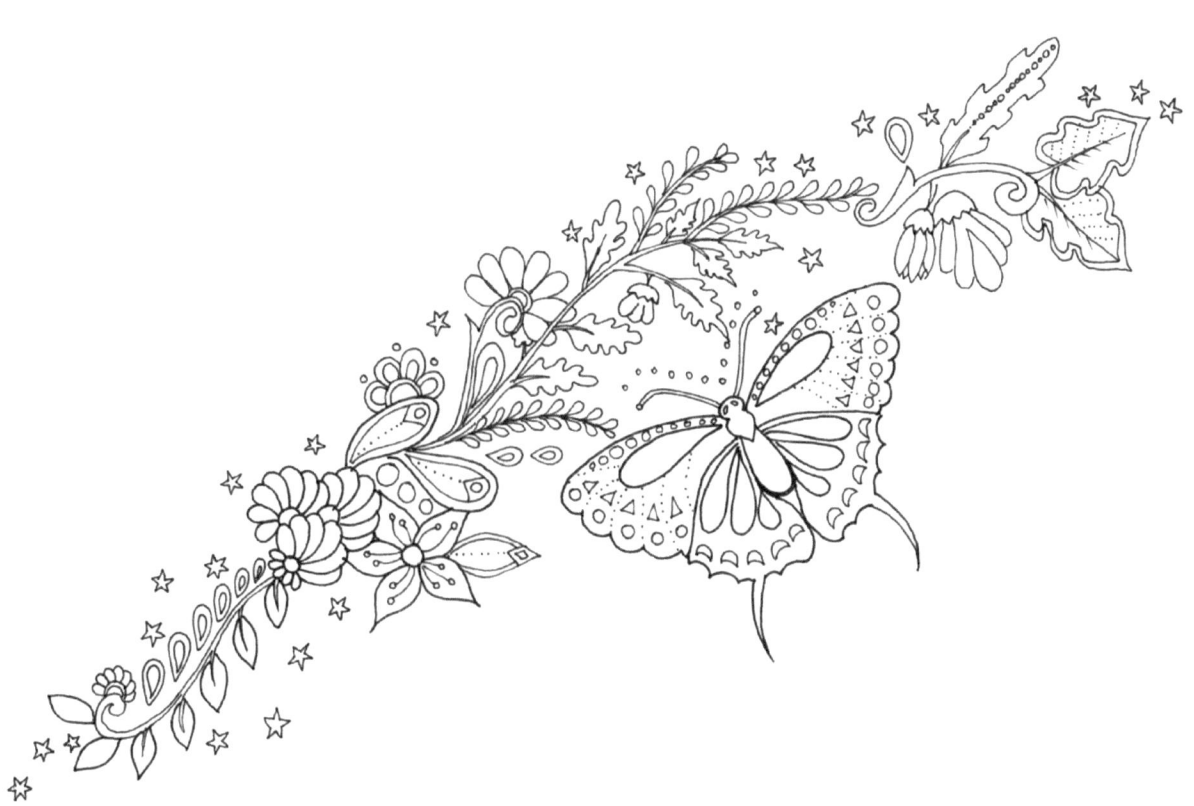

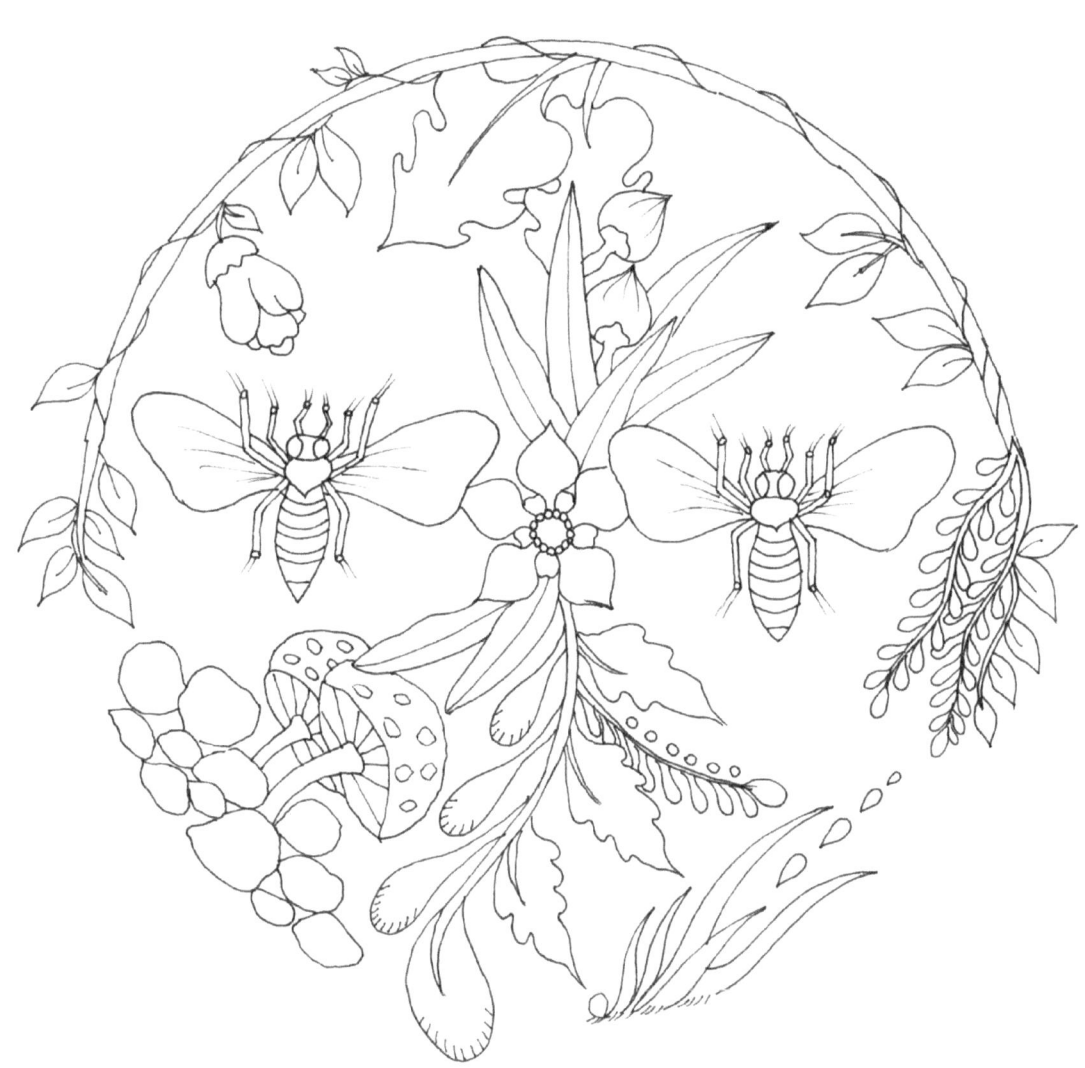

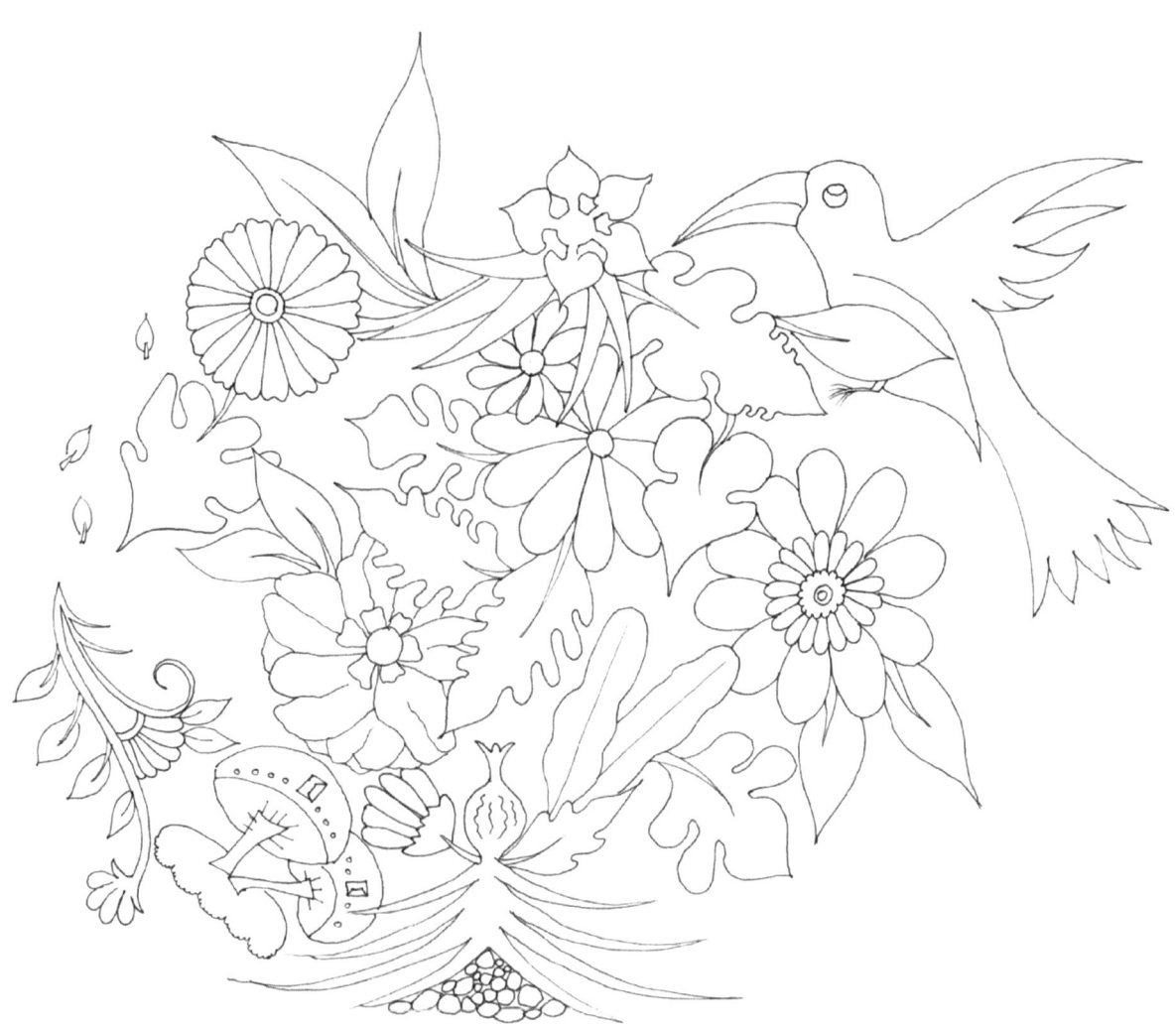

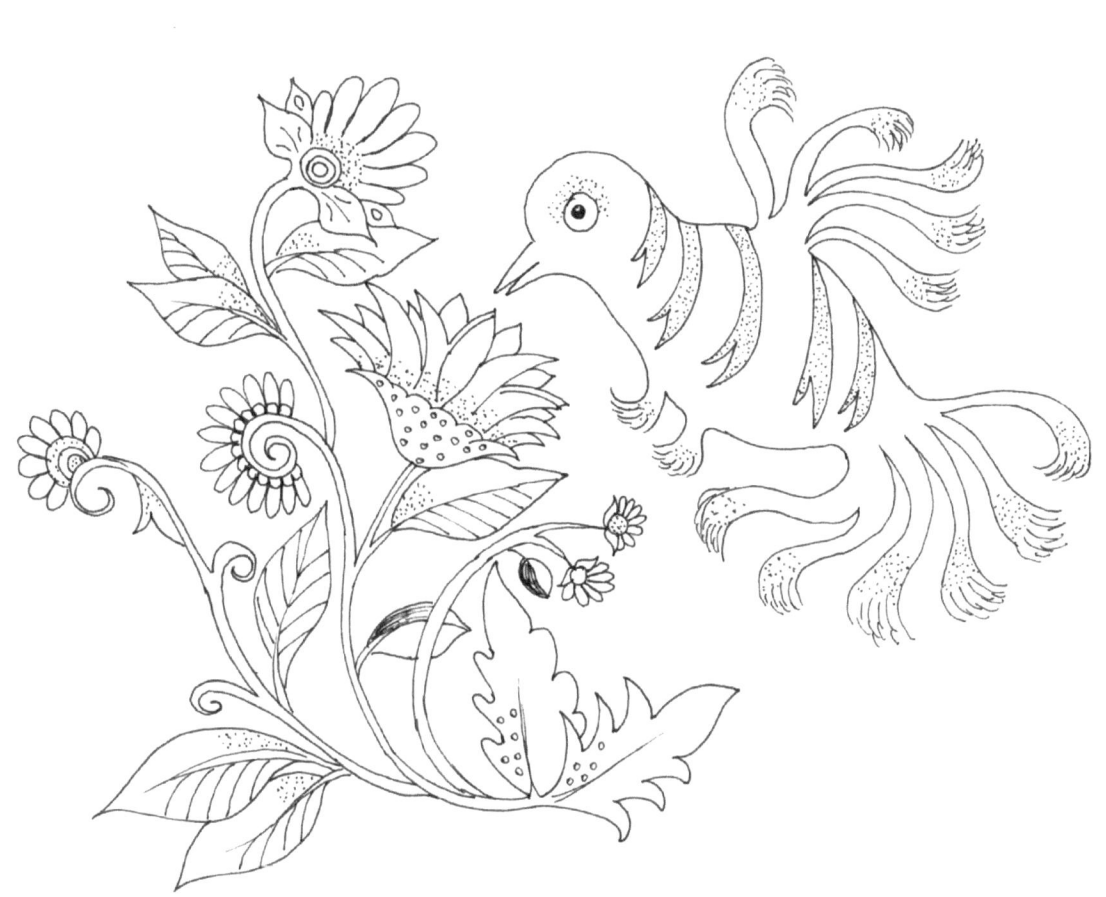

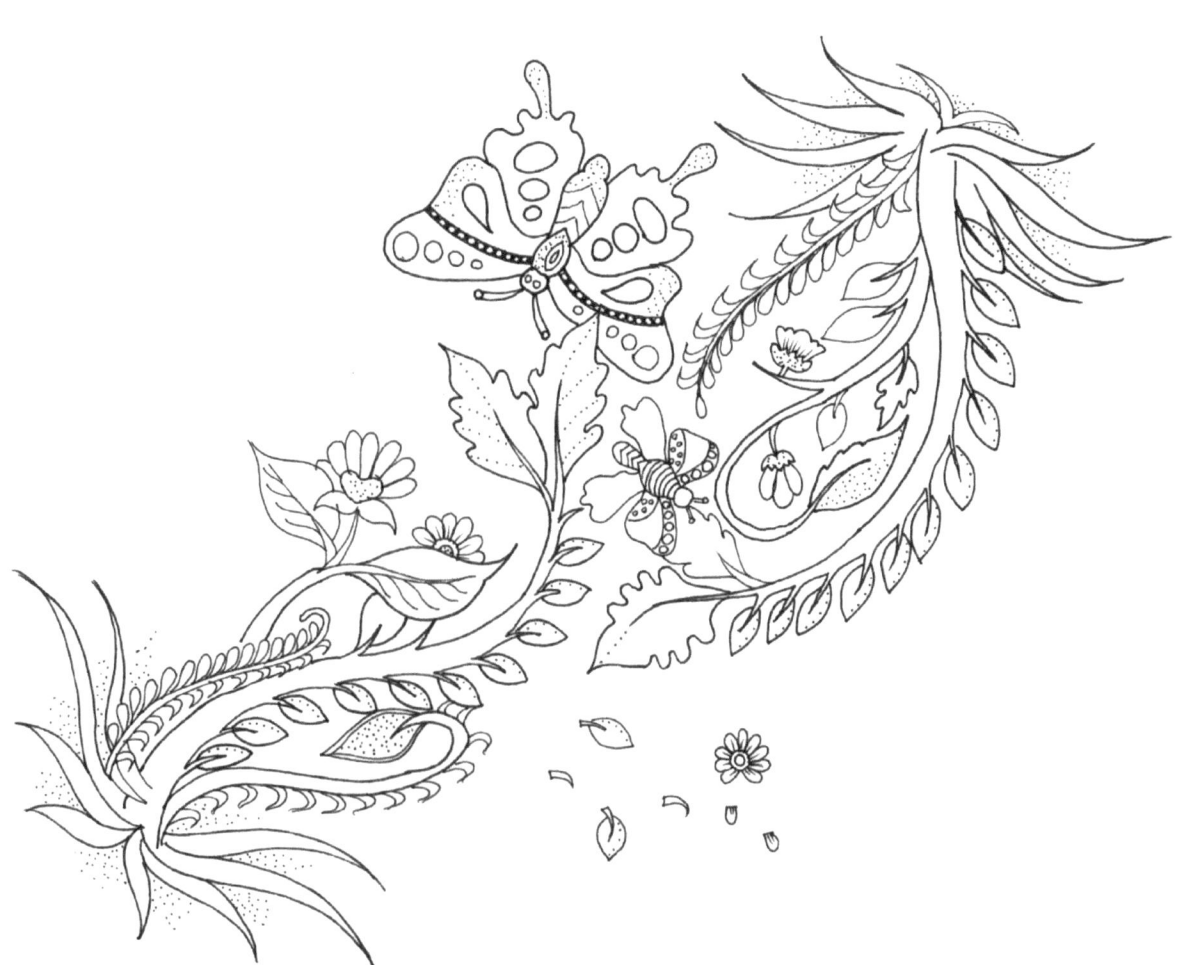

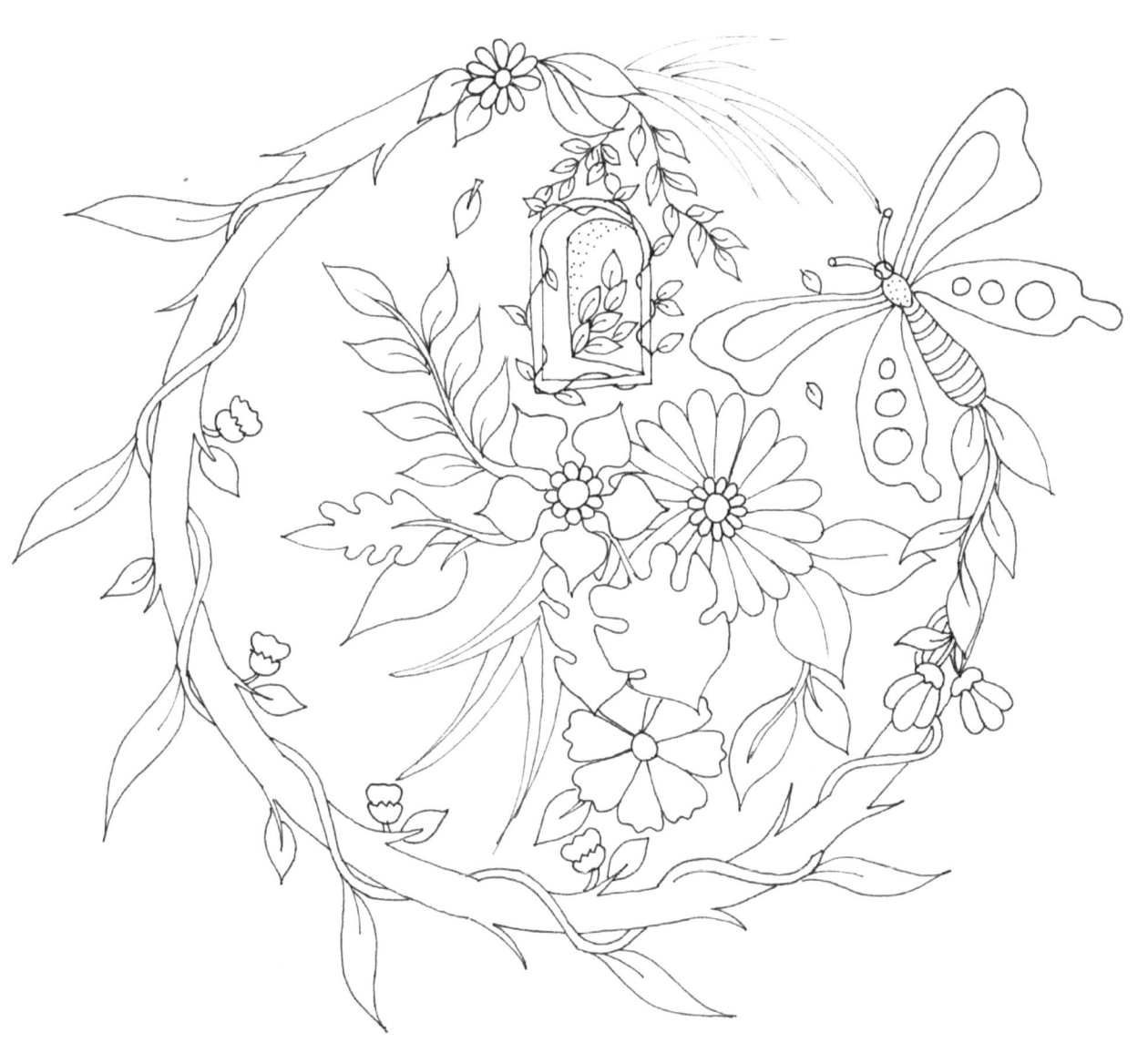

Art unlocks your true creative potential. Keep colouring and become an Artist.

#Authentikminds

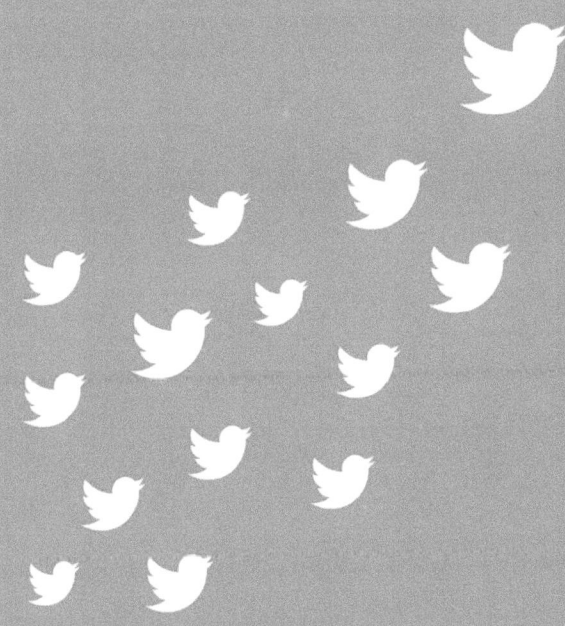

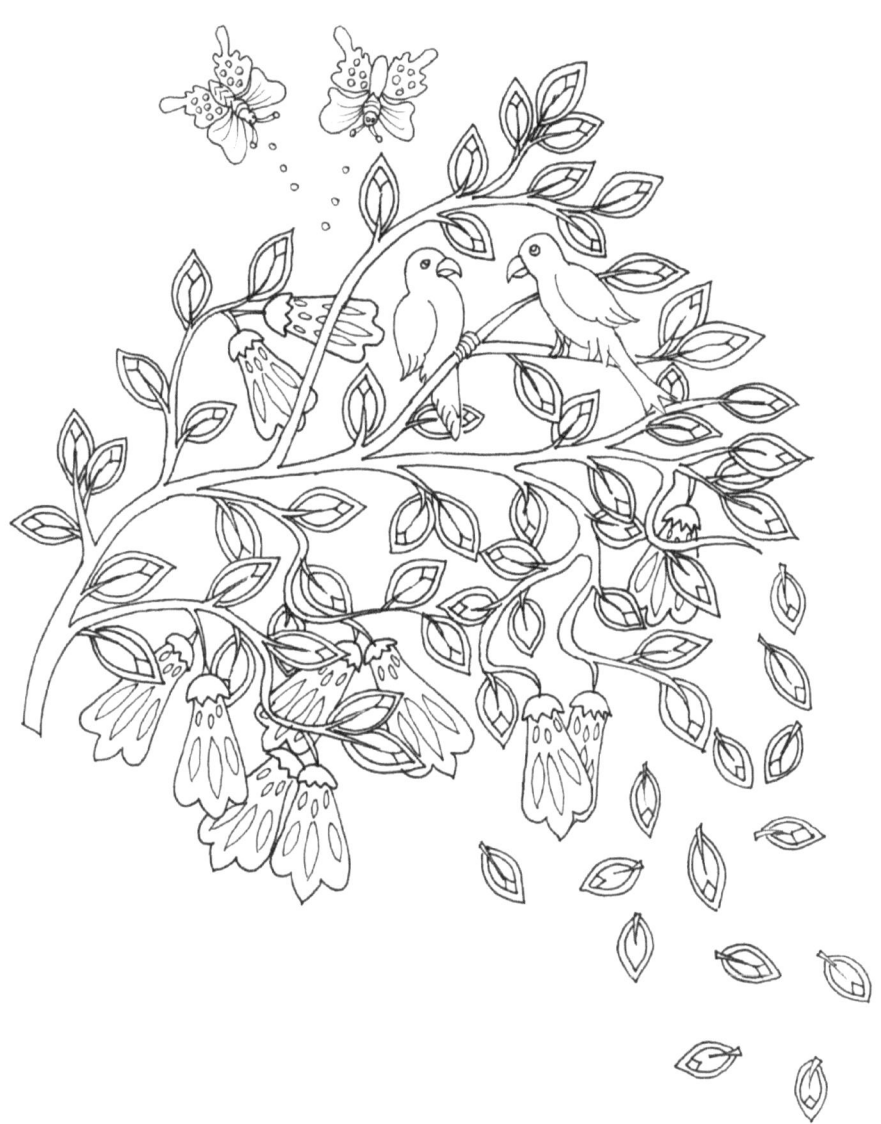

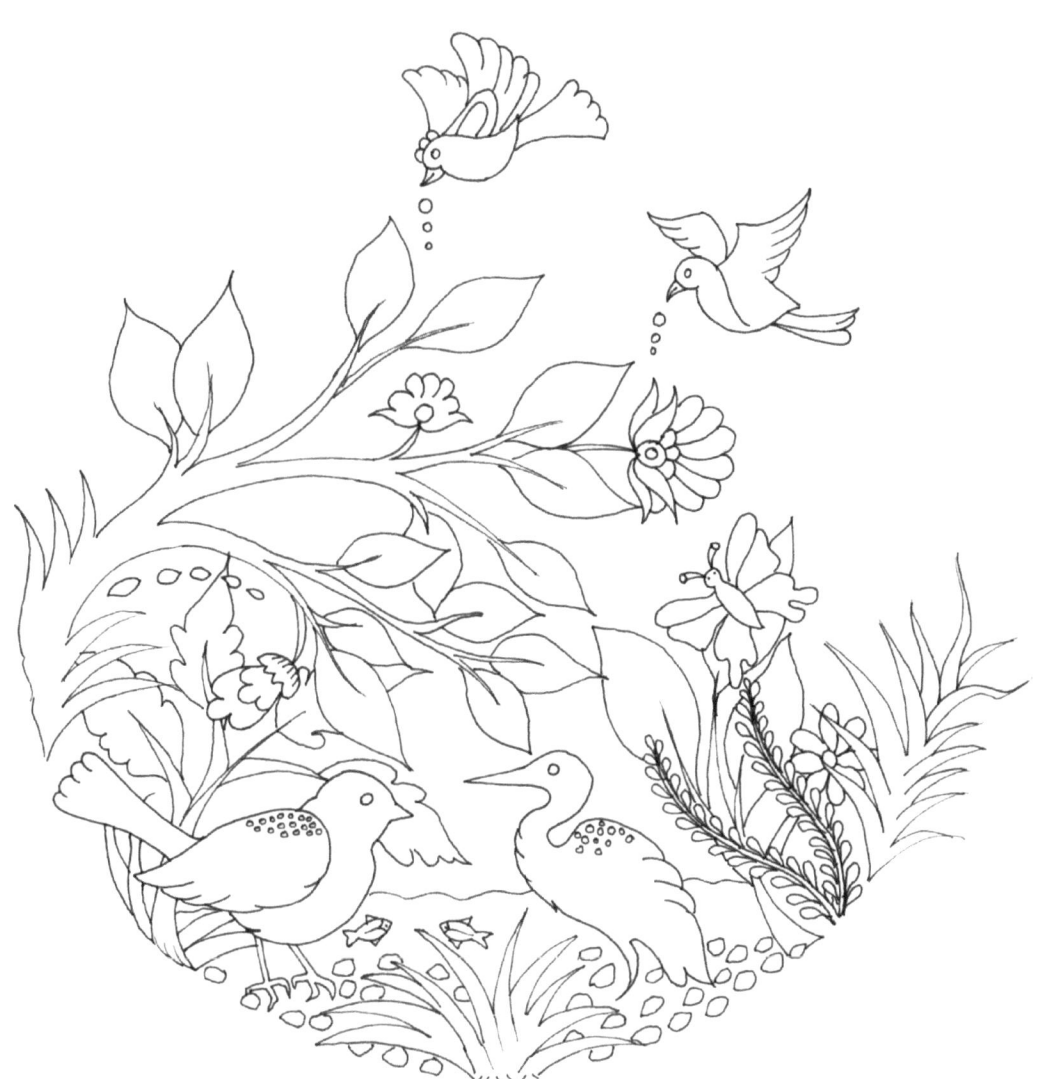

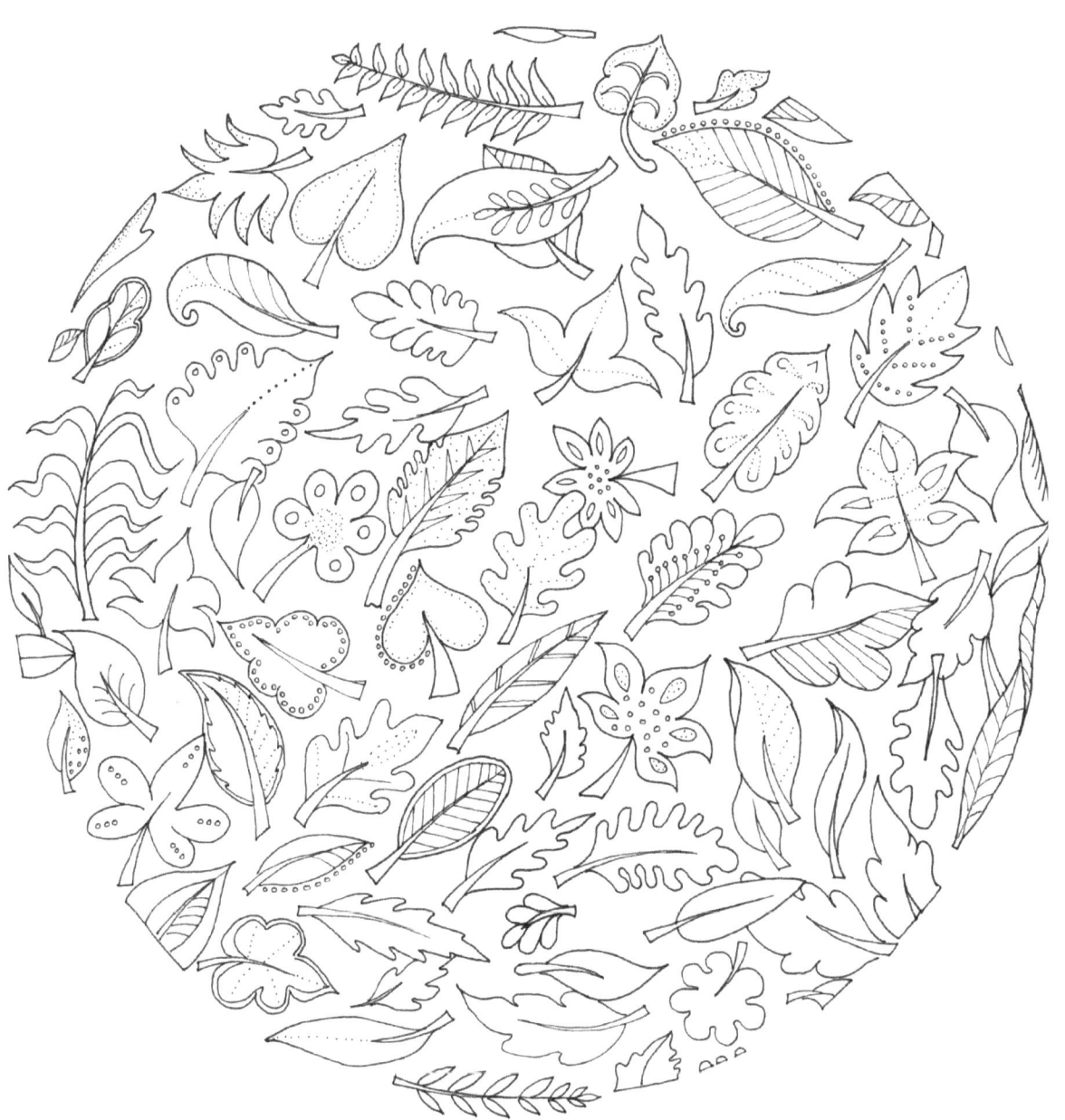

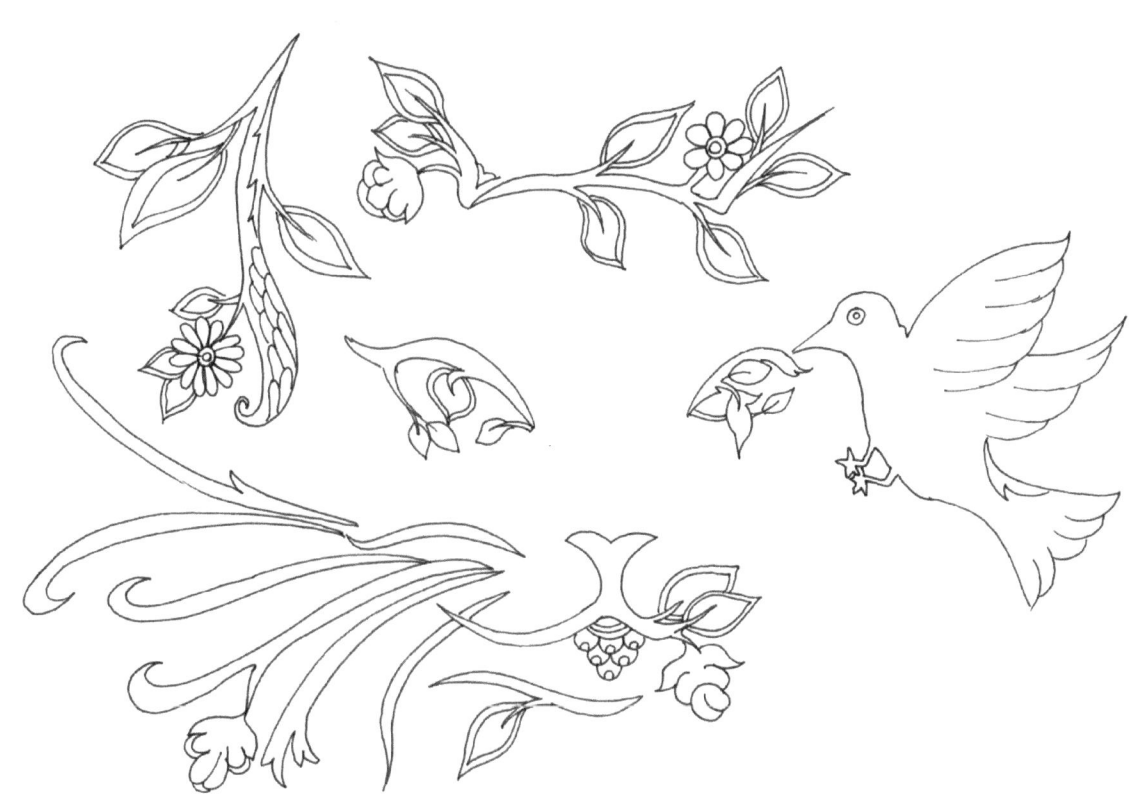

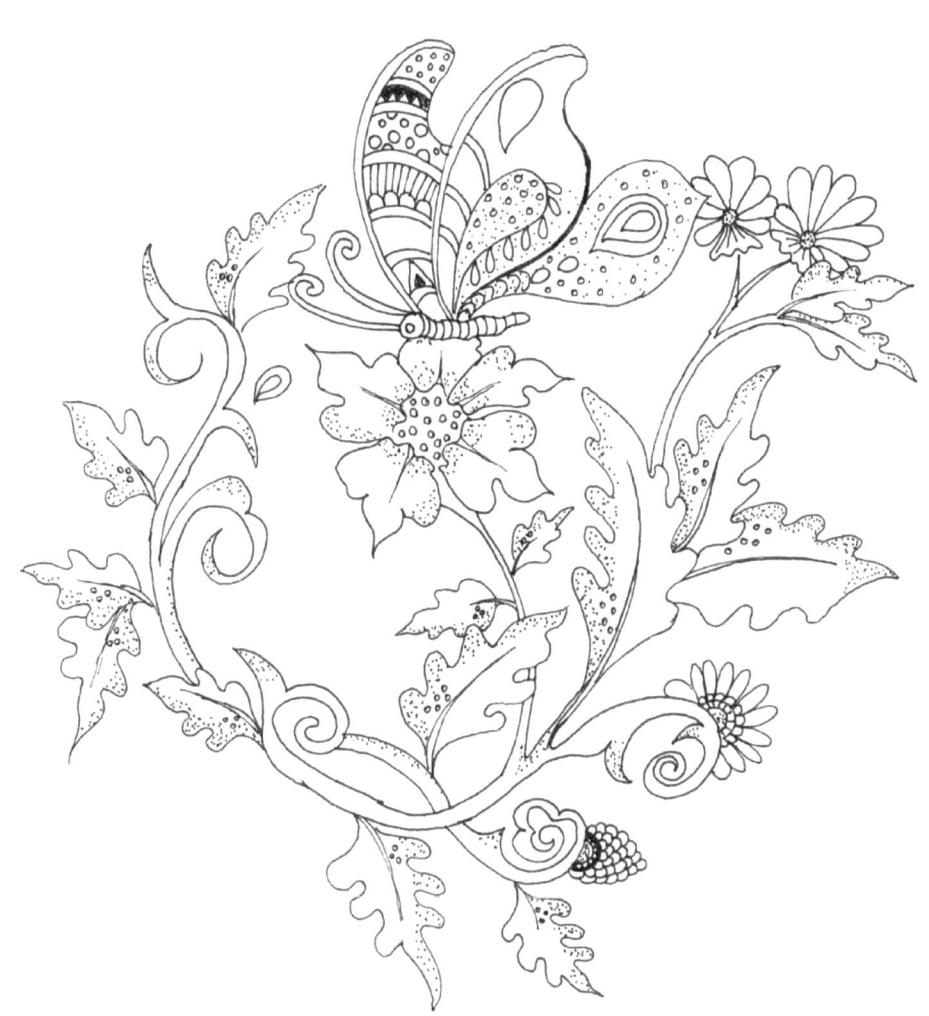

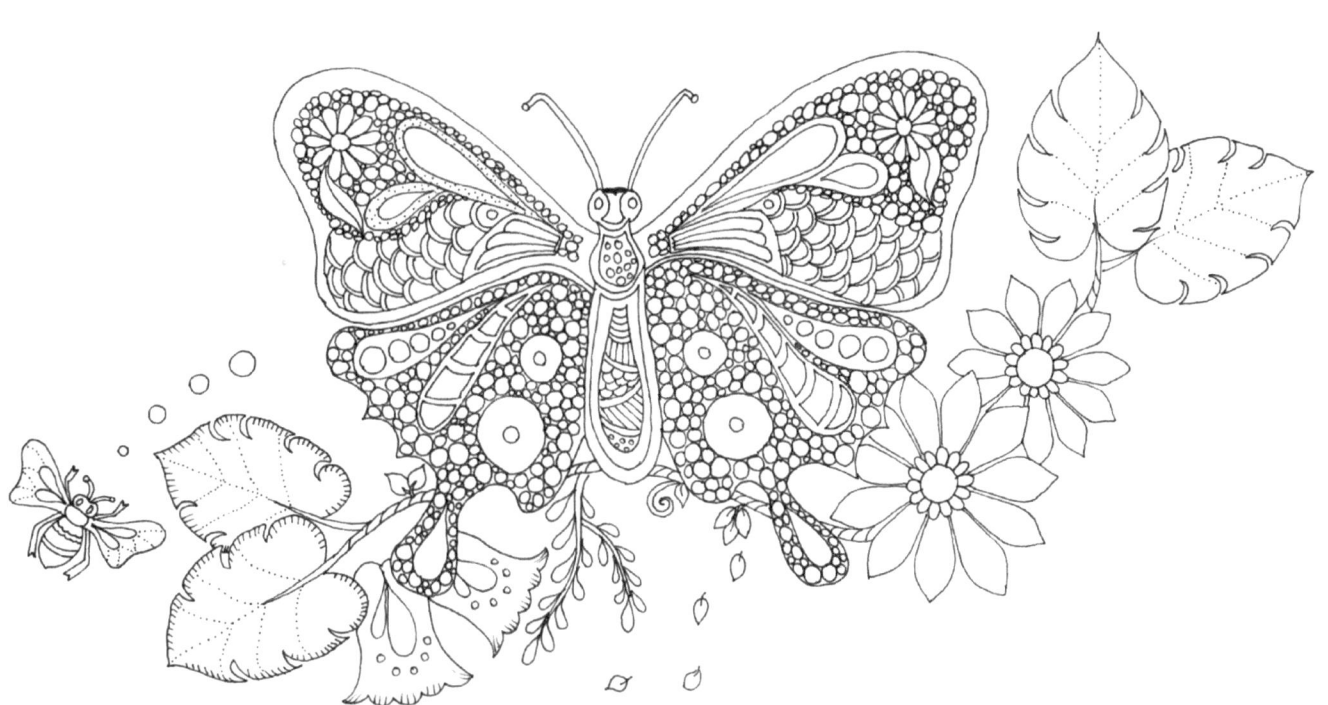

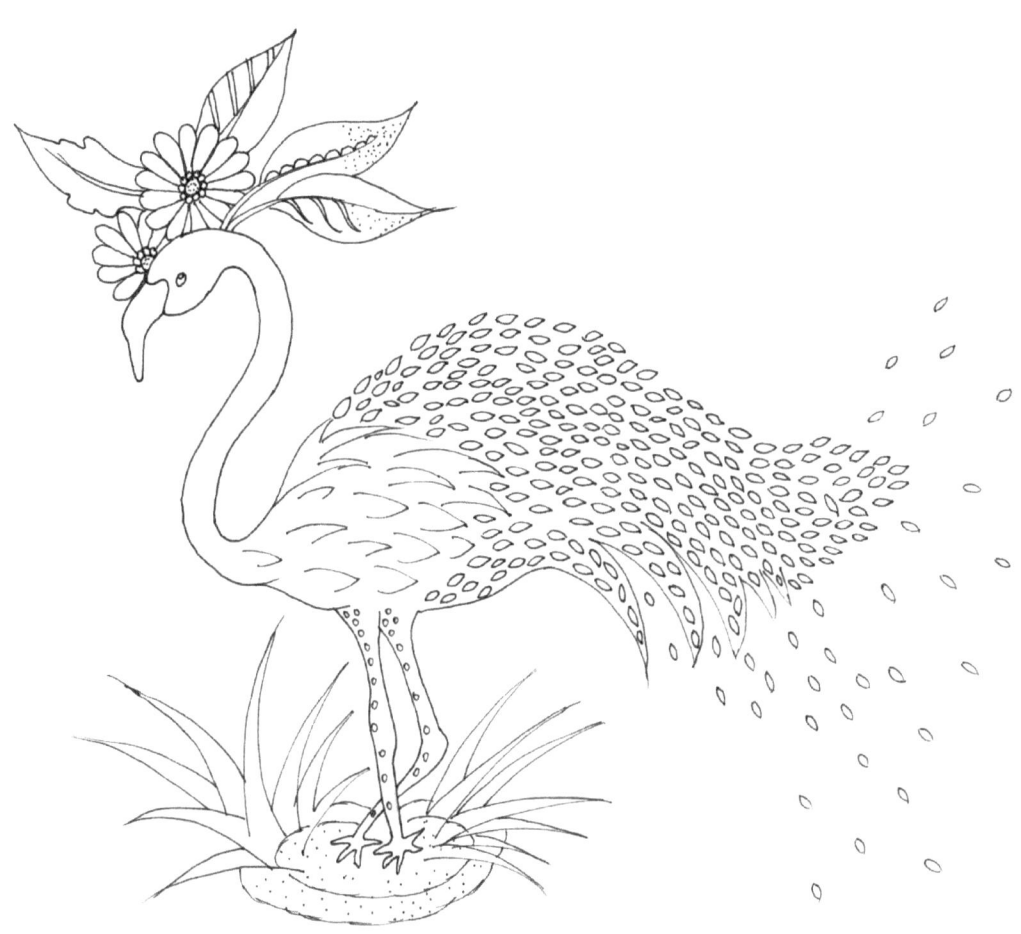

The fine art of human
relation is Smile.
Draw more to Smile more

#Authentikminds

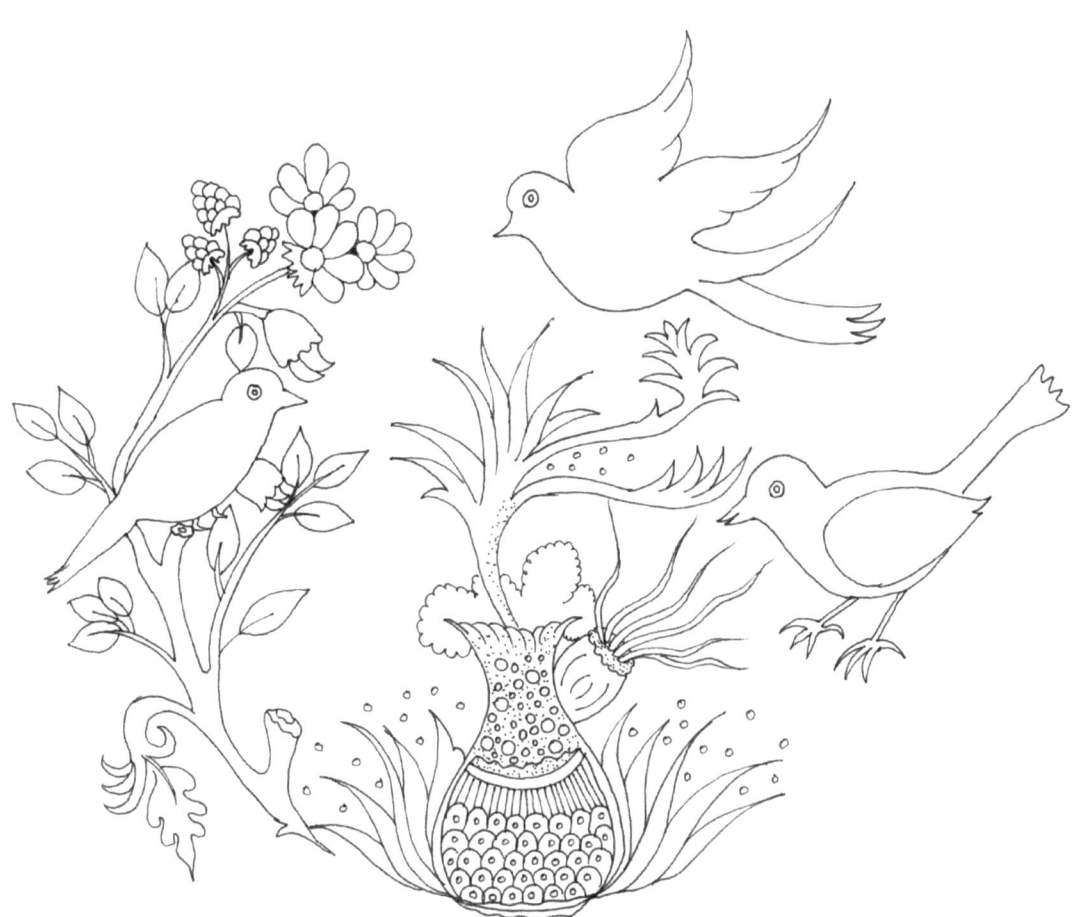

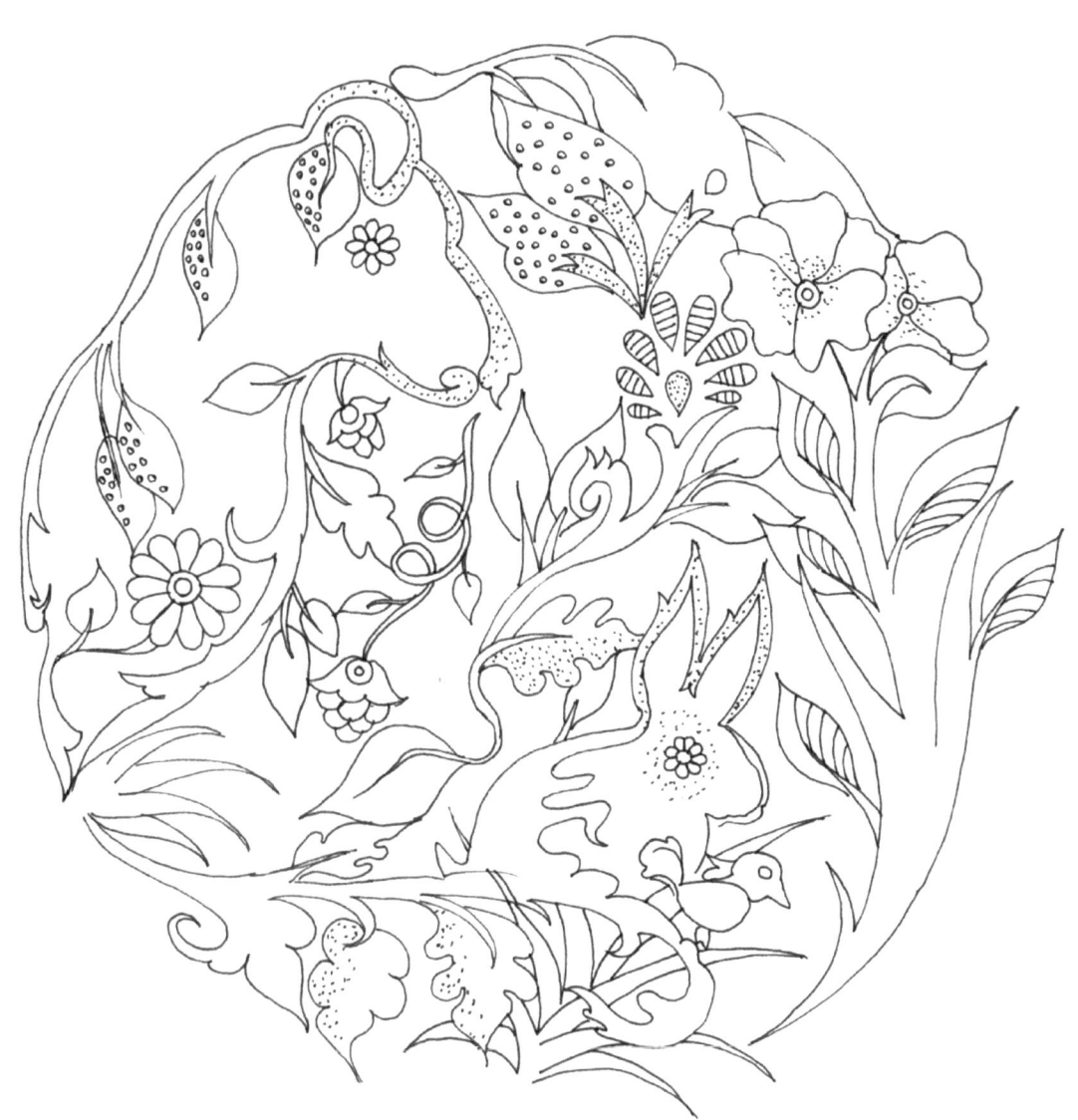

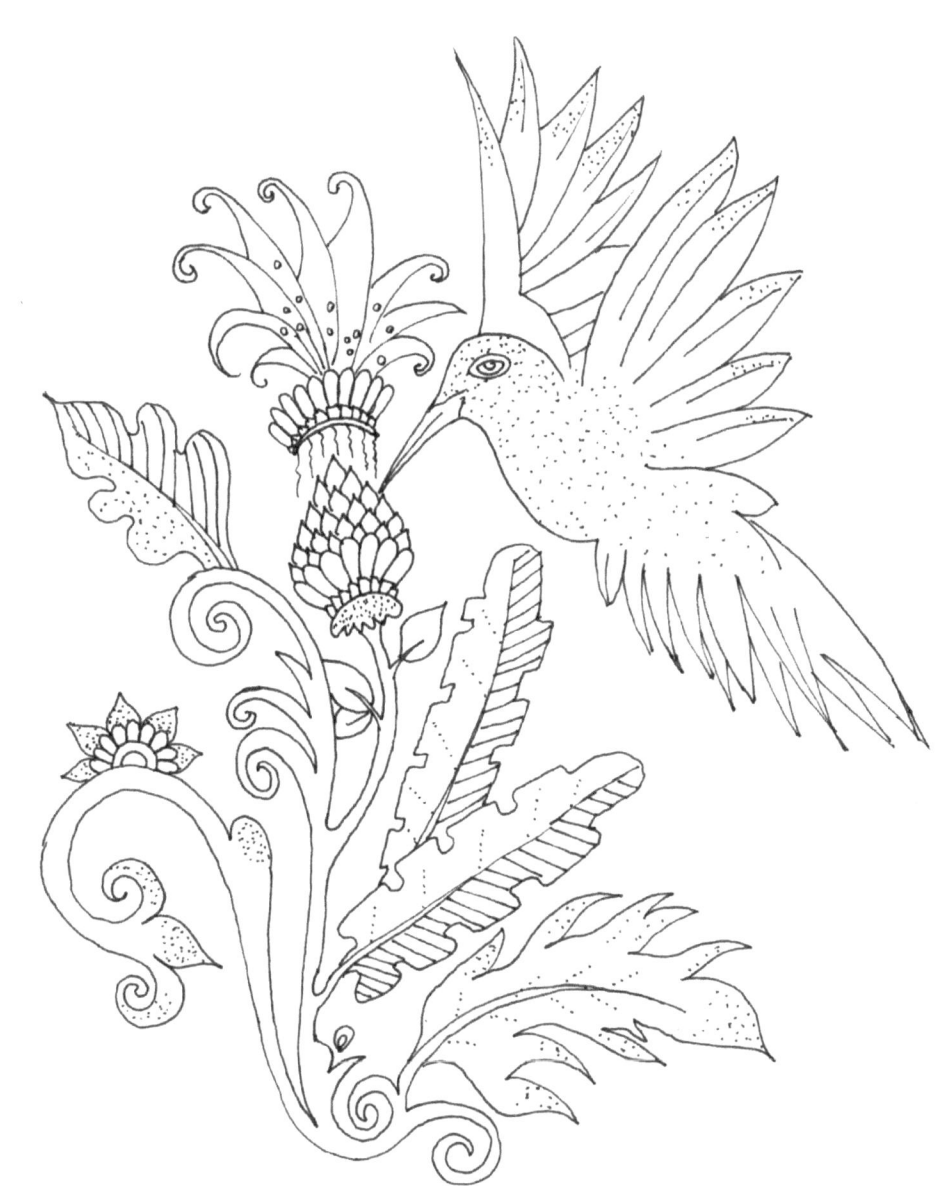

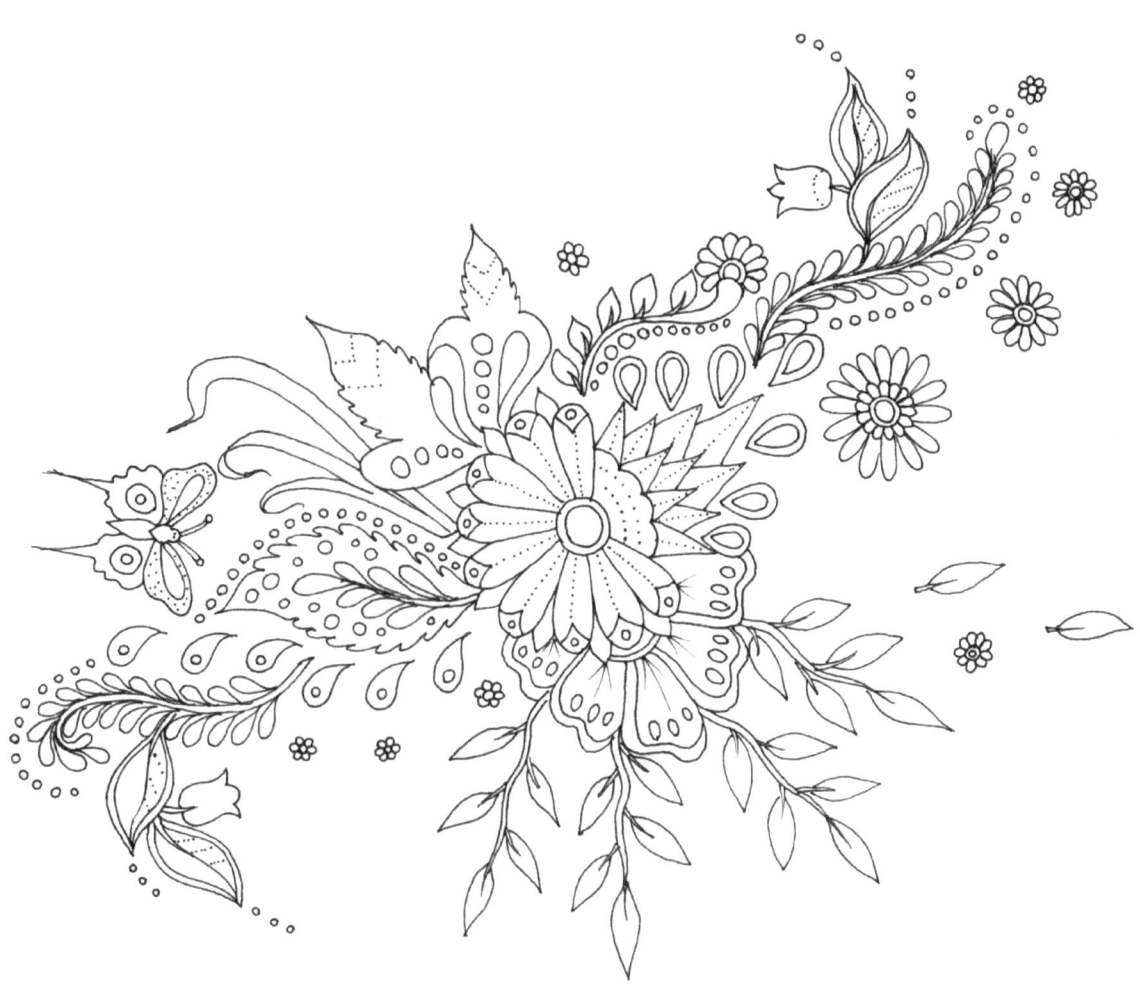

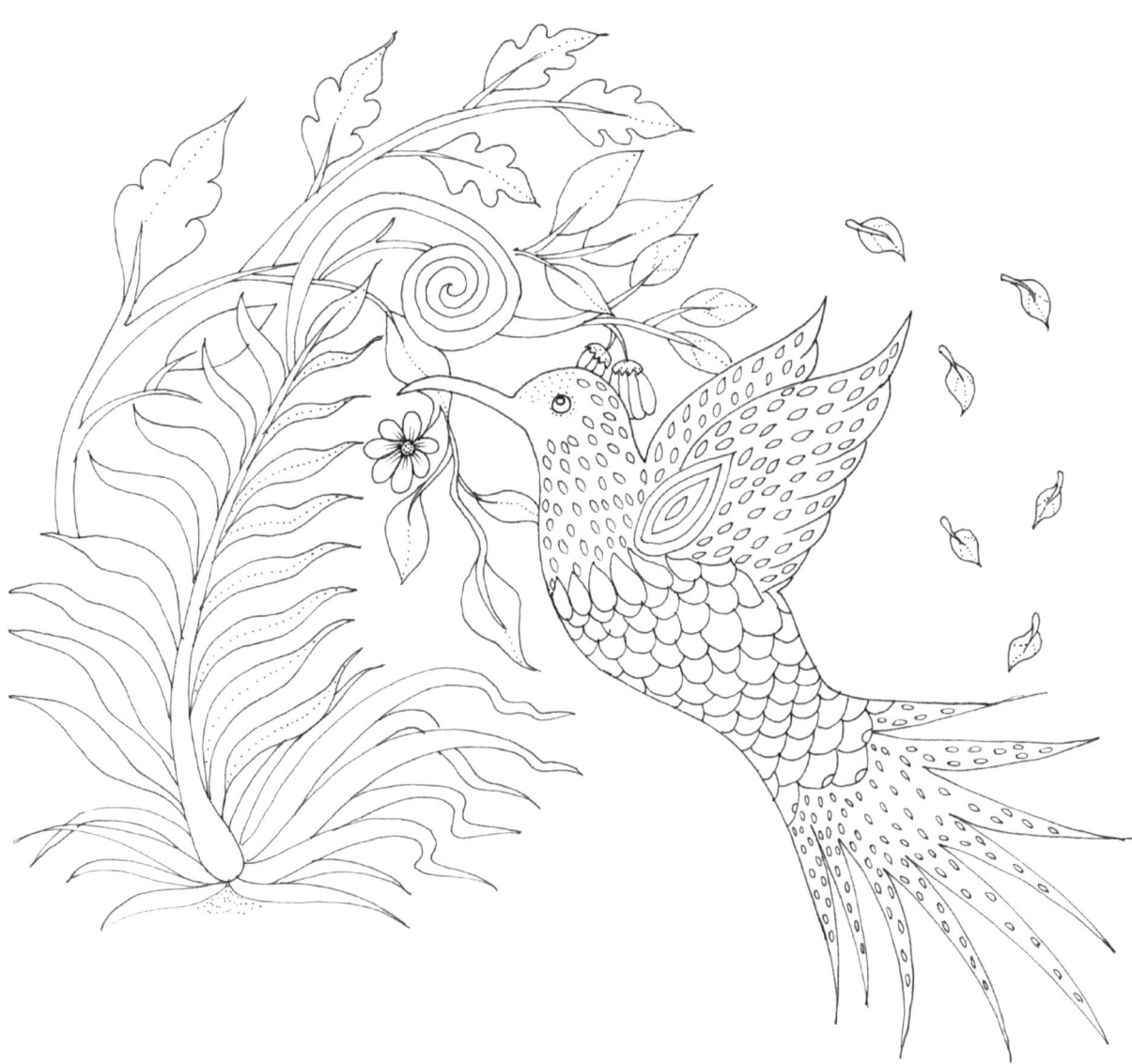

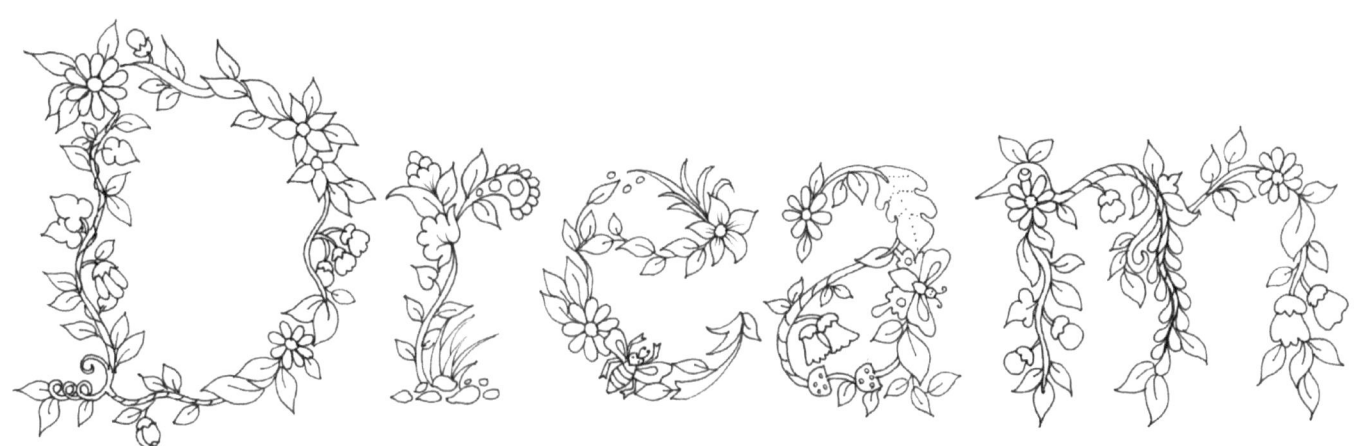

Author's Other Book
"Meditate through Mandala"

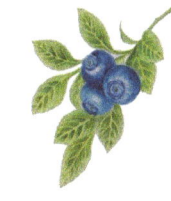
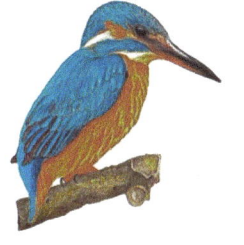
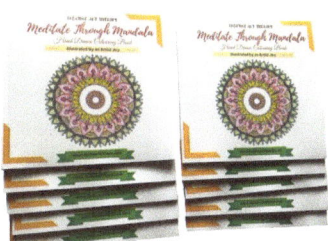
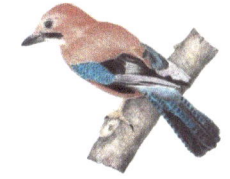

Visit Art Portfolio @ www.authentikminds.com

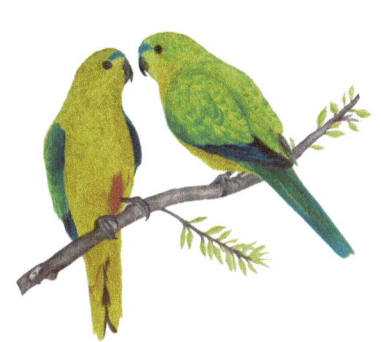
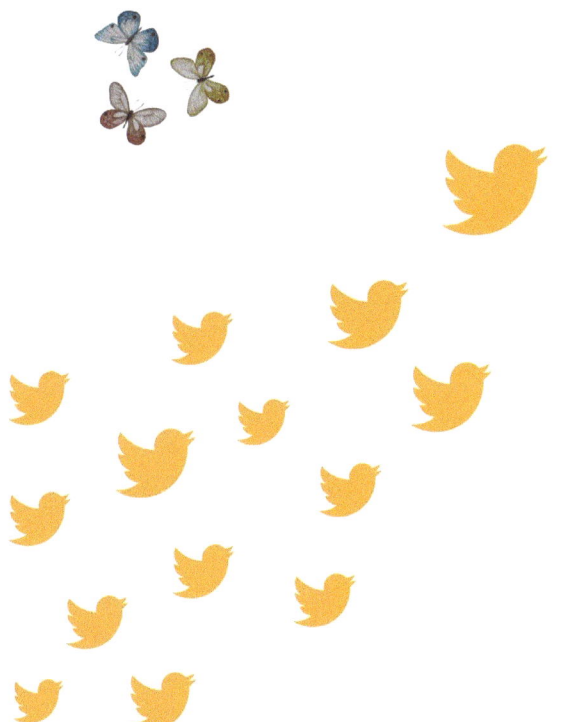
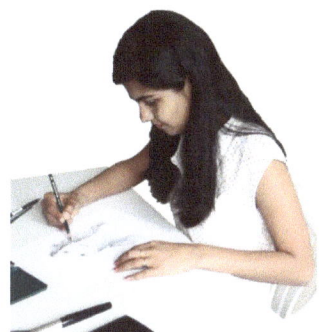

AuthentikMinds Creative Space

www.ingramcontent.com/pod-product-compliance
Lightning Source LLC
Chambersburg PA
CBHW041932240526
45473CB00034B/915